Tell me about...

Cycling

Published in 2010 by Evans Publishing Ltd,
2A Portman Mansions,
Chiltern St, London WIU 6NR

Editor: Nicola Edwards
Designer: D.R. Ink
All photographs by Wishlist except for page 6 Clive Rose/Getty Images; page 12 Bryn Lennon/Getty
Images; page 13 Feng Li/Getty Images; page 17 (t) Barry Durrant/Getty Images, (b) Shutterstock; page 19
Shutterstock; page 21 JAVIER SORIANO/AFP/Getty Images; page 22 iStock; page 23 JANEK
SKARZYNSKI/AFP/Getty Images; pp24-25 Shutterstock; page 26 Jasper Juinen/Getty Images; page 27
CARL DE SOUZA/AFP/Getty Images

British Library Cataloguing in Publication Data

Gifford, Clive.
  Cycling. -- (Tell me about sport)
  1. Cycling--Juvenile literature.
  I. Title II. Series
  796.6-dc22
  ISBN-13: 9780237541521

Printed in China.

The author and publisher would like to thank Kai Whyte, Emma Pitt, Alice Barnes and Reg Pay,
coach Andrew Pitt and Parker Park Velo for their help with the photographs for this book.

Contents

▲
Great Britain's Chris Hoy, Jason Kenny and Jamie Staff race around a banked velodrome track as they compete in the team track cycling event at the 2008 Olympics. Top sprinters can reach up to 70km/h.

Ever since bicycles were invented in the 1800s, people have loved riding them and racing them against others. Cycling has developed into a wide-ranging sport in which girls and boys can take part.

Some cycle races and competitions are held on an oval track called a velodrome. Others are held on roads for individual riders or giant groups of racers. Mountain bikes with sturdy frames and wheels are ridden off-road over special courses or along rocky, dusty or grassy trails.

You don't have to cycle competitively to enjoy riding. Using a bike is a healthy way to travel to school or work. Regular cycling will boost your fitness, which is useful for other sports as well.

▲
A boy rides a mountain bike with chunky tyres. For longer distances, cyclists often use touring bikes with narrower wheels and a lighter frame.

Millions of people cycle every day. Some people join a cycling club to improve their ability. It is great fun to cycle through beautiful scenery on roads and tracks and exciting to ride off-road. Cycling gives you the freedom to explore an area – and it's good for the environment, too.

▲ These cyclists are practising their steering and balance by tackling a simple slalom course at their local cycling club.

▼ Riders race over a BMX course. Their bikes are built strongly to withstand bumps and crashes and they wear full-face helmets.

Bike parts and tools

Bikes come in many different types, but nearly all have similar important parts. Cyclists sit on a saddle and turn two pedals with their feet. The movement of the pedals drives the chainwheel and chain. The chain is connected to the back wheel via a gear sprocket. Pedalling drives the rear wheel round and moves the bike forward.

Bike frames used to be made of steel but most are now made of aluminium tubing, which means they are light but strong. The bike's handlebars are connected to the front forks which hold the front wheel in place.

▼ This racing bike has dropped handlebars, a lightweight frame and narrow wheels with smooth tyres. It is used for riding at good to high speeds on roads and tracks.

Basic tools

puncture repair kit

spanner for adjusting nuts and bolts

hex keys for adjusting bolts

▲ Keeping your bike clean and in good repair helps all of its parts work better.

The levers that control the brakes are part of the handlebars. When a cyclist brakes, blocks of rubber touch the rim of the wheel. This creates friction which slows the wheel down. Check your brake blocks often to make sure they are not rubbing on the rim when the brakes are not on.

To keep your bike working well, it's important to know how its key parts work and how to look after and repair them. Spending a little time regularly to keep your bike in good shape will save you time and money later.

Cycling safety

Cycling can be risky, especially for a beginner. Make sure you learn to ride well. Ask your parents and teachers about taking bike safety or cycling proficiency classes. These will teach you all about road signs and rules as well as showing you how to ride better.

▼
This cyclist is wearing a helmet, elbow pads and padded cycling gloves to protect these vulnerable areas in case of a crash.

Build your experience gradually and always cycle with an adult at a gentle speed on your first journeys on roads. If you are unsure about how to cross a busy junction, you can pull into the pavement, get off your bike and wheel it across a pedestrian crossing.

Cycle safely

- Don't wear an mp3 player or use a mobile phone while cycling.
- Do keep a good distance (at least three bike lengths) from traffic in front of you.
- Don't ride 'no-handed', carry a passenger or balance objects on your bike.
- Do obey traffic lights and other signs.

Whenever you cycle, make sure you wear a good cycle helmet. This will protect you from serious head injuries. A helmet should fit securely with the chin strap tight but comfortable. Your clothing and shoelaces shouldn't be loose enough to flap around. If they do, there's a risk they may become caught up in the chain and this could cause you to crash.

A bag fitted to your bike or a small rucksack worn on your back can hold any items you may need when you go on a longer ride. These include lightweight waterproof clothing, water, a map and sunblock if the weather is warm.

▲
Bike thefts occur every day. Guard against losing your bike by locking it up securely to a fixed object and taking clip-off parts such as lights with you.

▶
These cyclists are riding on a cycle lane through their local park. They wear bright clothing so that they are clearly visible. If the weather turns gloomy they will switch on their bike lights.

Cycling superstars

Top cyclists like Lance Armstrong, Victoria Pendleton, Sir Chris Hoy and Jeannie Longo-Ciprelli are international sporting stars. But behind the glamour and fame, there lies a huge amount of hard work. Top cyclists fight fatigue and exhaustion to push themselves to the limit.

Cyclists have to train incredibly hard for maximum fitness and match this with a carefully-planned diet. They have to deal with the frustrations that come with injuries.

▼ American cycling legend Lance Armstrong on his way to winning the 2005 Tour de France, his seventh victory in a row.

Despite wearing helmets, a crash at very high race speeds can still cause serious injuries. In early 2009, Sir Chris Hoy crashed and injured his hip, ending his entire year's racing.

Some top cyclists switch between different forms of racing. Britain's Shanaze Reade is a world champion on muddy BMX courses with their sharp turns, dips and bumps. She also rides on the track and in both 2007 and 2008 won the world team sprint championship with Victoria Pendleton.

Talented young cyclists do not enter professional cycling for the money. Although the exact amounts are often kept secret, most pro cyclists do not earn large sums even if they are part of a successful racing team. Only a handful of the most famous such as Lance Armstrong can earn large sums through endorsing products in adverts.

Cycling legends

In 2008, the amazing Jeannie Longo-Ciprelli appeared at her seventh Olympic games in a row. She has won Olympic gold as well as an amazing 12 World Championships on the road and the track.

In the 1999 Tour de France, Lance Armstrong completed the 3,870 km course including its gruelling hill climbs at an average speed of over 40.2km/h.

▼ Shanaze Reade (right) leads in a BMX World Cup race in 2007, an event she would win. Shanaze first got into BMX racing at the age of ten and bought her first bike for just one pound!

Riding and cornering

▲ This rider checks for any possible traffic before starting to ride. Always use a low gear (see page 16) when you start off. This makes it much easier to build up a little speed.

Start any ride by checking your path is clear in front of and behind you. Look over your shoulder to check before you push off and put both feet on the pedals.

Make sure your riding position allows you to stay balanced and comfortable. Your arms should be bent a little at the elbow and your head must be up with your eyes scanning the road ahead.

Try to keep both your hands on the handlebars except when you're signalling or reaching down for your water bottle. Keep your fingers on or close to the brake levers so that you are ready to apply the brakes.

Unless it is an emergency, you should brake gently. Try to start braking well before you need to

▲ Your riding position should allow you to reach the brake levers and other controls on the handlebars easily.

▲ Use the ball of your foot on the pedal which will make pedalling easier and less tiring on your legs.

stop. If you brake suddenly and sharply, you risk losing control and skidding or, worse, flying over the handlebars. Use both brakes evenly, applying the back brake slightly before the front.

To make slight changes of direction, you just turn the handlebars gently. For a bigger turn, you need to lean gently into the turn, keeping your

▶

This cyclist leans and steers through a corner. As she leaves the corner, she will get back into an upright position and pedal away.

inside pedal up so that it doesn't clip the ground. Let the handlebars follow the direction of your lean.

Gears and hills

It's important to know how to use your gears so that you can travel smoothly up and down slopes or hills. Low gears make your back wheel turn less for each turn of the pedals. This makes the bike travel forward more slowly. A higher gear turns your back wheel more and so increases your speed.

Use your gears to build up or slow down your speed when you are cycling on level ground. Cycling at a steady rate uses up less energy. When you're cycling up or down a slope, you have to change gears smoothly to keep pedalling at the same rate.

▶
BMX bikes have no gears to change up or down when you are tackling a hill. This rider has to pump his legs up and down on the pedals to keep up his speed as he rides uphill.

When you're cycling uphill, try to keep your bottom on the saddle with your weight over the back wheel. This helps keep you stable as you pump your legs to turn the pedals. Take care when you're riding down the other side of a hill. Keep your speed under control and stay balanced by shifting your body weight over the back wheel.

▲ Top cyclists on very steep hills often get out of the saddle, and stand on their pedals to generate extra power. This is called honking and is very tiring unless you are extremely fit.

▼ It is very important to get your weight over the back wheel when travelling downhill. Keep your speed controlled by pumping your back brake on and off repeatedly.

Rough riding

Riding off-road on a mountain or hybrid bike can offer real thrills. You have the freedom to explore interesting new trails and places but you must stay alert for possible obstacles and dangers at all times.

As well as obstacles, such as logs and rocks, and ditches at ground level, you need to be aware of bushes and overhanging tree branches that could catch your head or body. If there is an area of water ahead, stop and check how deep it is first, before attempting to cross it.

▶

Padded cycling gloves help cushion your hands from the bumps and jolts of riding off-road. They can also stop blisters forming and grazes should you fall off your bike.

▲ This cyclist performs a small, controlled wheelie. He pulls back on the handlebars to lift the front wheel. To get it back down, he brings his body weight forward.

It's important to keep the wheels turning as you ride through loose surfaces such as gravel, sand or a thin layer of mud. Staying in the lower gears will allow you to pedal continuously to keep your wheels moving.

Respect the countryside code when you're cycling in rural areas. Close any gates you open, don't leave rubbish behind and keep a clear distance between yourself and any animals or people walking nearby.

▲
This biker uses a low gear so that he can move forward slowly and keep his balance as he steers his way through rocks and stones.

Road racing

There are many different types of cycling competition. Many are held on roads for amateurs and professional cyclists. Road cyclists use very lightweight bikes with dropped handlebars so they can cycle along roads at high speed, often at well over 50km/h.

▼ The cyclist (left) has been tucked in behind a rival. This is called slipstreaming and means he uses less energy than the rider at the front to move forward. Deciding to overtake, he pulls out to the side of the lead rider and pedals hard to pass his rival. Cyclists often share the work of riding in front.

Junior riders aren't allowed to race on open roads with car traffic. Some can race on roads that have been closed off to other traffic. A criterium is one type of closed road race. It is a short race of a few kilometres on a route through a town.

Many races on open or closed roads have a massed start with all the riders in a huge group. The winner is the first rider to cross the finish line. Other races are time trials, in which competitors set off one by one with gaps in between each of them. Every cyclist is timed and the cyclist with the quickest time is the winner.

Other competitions on roads are made up of a number of different stages. These may include special stages such as steep hill or mountain climbs or time trials. The most famous stage races are the three Grand Tours competitions – the Tour de France, Italy's Giro D'Italia and Spain's Vuelta a España.

Grand Tours

The 2009 Tour de France won by Alberto Contador contained 21 stages in 23 days, with the longest stage measuring a huge 211.5km.

Italians have won the Giro D'Italia 65 times. The next most successful nation is Belgium with seven victories, five of them by cycling legend Eddie Mercyx.

The 1984 Vuelta a España course was 3593km long and took more than 90 hours of cycling to complete. Yet Éric Caritoux won by just six seconds!

▲ Many road races end with an exciting massed sprint to the finish line. Here, Peter Velis from Slovakia wins the sprint finish at the Road Racing World Championships while other riders crash behind him.

Track races

Track racing has been popular for more than a hundred years. Tracks are mostly 250 metres long and have steeply angled or banked sides. They are found indoors or outdoors in a centre called a velodrome.

A wide range of races are held in velodromes. These include sprints between two competing riders and time trials in which cyclists must compete a set distance on their own in the fastest possible time.

▼ A team of track cyclists competes in a team pursuit race (see page 23). The bikes have carbon fibre wheels which help make them incredibly light – often as little as 7kg.

In pursuit races, individual cyclists or teams of four start a race on opposite sides of the track. They then race over the complete distance (usually 4000m in team pursuit and men's individual and 3000m in women's individual pursuit) or until one rider catches up with a rival.

One of the strangest track cycling events is the keirin. Invented in Japan, cyclists in the eight lap race follow a motorbike called a derny. The derny winds up its speed before leaving the cyclists to sprint the last two and a half laps of the track.

Track cyclists compete on unusual bikes which are very narrow and have no gears or brakes. They also have handlebar positions that face forward, helping the rider form an extreme tucked position for maximum speed. Top sprinters can achieve astonishing speeds of around 80km/h.

▼ British track cyclist and Olympic gold medallist Victoria Pendleton (left) moves up on Willy Kanis from the Netherlands on her way to winning the final of the sprint race at the 2009 World Championships.

Mountain biking

Mountain biking has many different types of competition. In freestyle events riders perform tricks similar to skateboarders. Trailquests are like orienteering competitions on bikes. Riders use a map and a compass to reach a series of checkpoints.

Cross-country races are the most well-known type of mountain bike competition. They are tests of endurance, speed and technical skill. Competitors race a number of laps of a difficult course full of climbs, drops, streams, ditches, tree logs and other obstacles. At the Olympics, the men's course is 40-50km long and the women's course is 30-40km.

▼ A mountain biker flies high after leaping up over a ridge. He wrestles for control of his bike so he can make a safe landing.

▼ This mountain biker weaves his way through a rocky trail. He keeps his weight over his back wheel to stay well balanced on his bike.

▲ These riders are pedalling hard during a mountain bike marathon competition over long distances in Kazakhstan.

Four-cross, also known as 4X, is a fast, furious race between four riders down a steep course with sharp jumps and turns. Downhill races are time trials in which each rider is timed as they travel down the course on their own.

Mountain bike trials are tests of riders' balance and control of their machine. Competitors have to get their bikes through a tough course full of obstacles, large and small, as cleanly as possible. Penalty points are added for mistakes such as a dab – putting their foot down on the ground.

The world of cycling

Cycling competitions and championships vary greatly, reflecting the different ways in which people practise the sport. There are local events for amateur road, track or off-road riders right up to a number of different world cups and world championships.

Champion cyclists

In 2008, Bradley Wiggins became world champion in the team and individual pursuit track competitions and won the Olympic individual pursuit gold medal.

Champion mountain biker Anne-Caroline Chausson won the Downhill competition at the World Mountain Bike Championships an incredible nine times before switching to BMX bikes and winning gold at the 2008 Olympics.

At the 2008 UCI Track Cycling World Championships in Manchester, British cyclists won an amazing nine of the 18 events.

Top road racers are members of professional race teams and compete at the Grand Tours events as well as in series of road races. From 2009, points scored by good performances in 24 major races will count to a world ranking competition.

◀ Albert Contador (centre) wears the yellow jersey of the Tour de France race leader as he cycles through the mountains in the 2009 race.

▲ Anne-Caroline Chausson of France leads during the 2008 Olympics BMX final on her way to winning the gold medal in the event.

The Union Cycliste Internationale (UCI) organises a series of world championships for road racing, track racing, BMX and mountain biking. The UCI World Mountain Bike and Trials Championships began in 1990 and have been held every year since. The championships feature competitions for downhill, cross-country, trials, four-cross and an exciting team relay race.

Cycling events have been a feature of every Olympic Games and up until 1972, there was even a race for tandem bikes featuring two people. There are currently ten track cycling events as well as road races, mountain biking and, since 2008, BMX racing competitions for men and women. For many cyclists, competing in the Olympics and winning medals is the pinnacle of their career.

Where next?

These books and websites will help you learn more about cycling.

http://new.britishcycling.org.uk/
A major British website with lots of news, features and links about cycling all over the country.

http://www.ctc.org.uk
Home page of the Cyclists Touring Club, this organisation offers lots of information and routes to cycle.

http://www.bikeforall.net/index.php
A large source of information on all forms and aspects of cycling from saddle height to cycle safety and etiquette.

http://www.mikeandthebike.com/cycling.php#content
Play some simple games and read about eating well for cycling and some safety advice on this fun website for children.

http://www.bikeability.org.uk/
Head to this website for details of Bikeability courses in your area which will help you learn to ride really well.

http://news.bbc.co.uk/sport1/hi/other_sports/cycling/default.stm
The BBC's cycling webpages are packed full of news, a calendar of events and a great get involved section with lots of tips and information about the different cycle sports.

Books

Know Your Sport: Cycling – Paul Mason, Franklin Watts, 2008
An introduction to the different types of cycling you can enjoy.

A World Class Mountain Biker – Andrew Hamilton, Heinemann Library, 2005
A really interesting look at how champion mountain bikers train, prepare and race.

Cycling words

BMX short for bicycle motorcross, a type of cycling and cycle racing over a rough dirt course with bumps and dips

criterium a type of cycling race through the roads and streets of a town

dab putting your feet down in error while taking part in a trials competition

four-cross a type of race in which four mountain bikers race along a specially prepared course, usually downhill

honking standing up out of your saddle and on your pedals when climbing a steep hill to gain more power

keirin a type of track cycle race in which a motorbike (called a derny) paces the cyclists through the first laps

slipstreaming tucking in close behind another cyclist so that the air flows round smoothly

team pursuit a type of track cycle race in which teams of four riders pursue another team around the track, trying to complete the distance in the fastest time

time trials races in which riders start individually and race against the clock. The fastest rider over a set distance is the winner

velodrome an oval track, often indoors, with angled bends to help cyclists race faster

wheelies lifting the front wheel of the bike off the ground, for example to clear an obstacle

Index

Numbers in **bold** refer to pictures.